WeightWatchers®

pizza toppings
& pasta sauces

Liz Tri

SIMON & SCHUSTER
A VIACOM COMPANY

First published in Great Britain by Simon and Schuster, 1998
A Viacom Company

This edition produced for
The Book People Ltd
Hall Wood Avenue
Haydock
St Helens
WA11 9UL

First published 1998
Reprinted 2002

Simon & Schuster UK Ltd
Africa House
64–78 Kingsway
London WC2B 6AH

Design: Moore Lowenhoff
Cover design: Zoocity
Typesetting: Stylize
Photography: Karl Adamson
Styling: Jo Harris
Food preparation: Shirley Gill

ISBN 0-68481-953-8

Printed in Hong Kong

Recipe notes:
Egg size is medium, unless otherwise stated.
Vegetables are medium-sized, unless otherwise stated.
It is very important to use proper measuring spoons, not cutlery, for spoon measures.
1 tablespoon = 15 ml; 1 teaspoon = 5 ml
Dried herbs can be substituted for fresh ones, but the flavour may not always
be as good. Halve the fresh-herb quantity stated in the recipe.

Vegetarian recipes:
Ⓥ shows the recipe is vegetarian.

Contents

Introduction

Pizza originated in Italy, but it has become a truly international food, enjoyed by people all over the world and is without a doubt one of the most popular dishes around. Pizza is very versatile and adaptable, so it's fun to make and experiment with. It is also a convenient meal in itself; the bread base, which is usually topped with a variety of meat and vegetables and then covered in cheese, is filling and a favourite family treat. Hot melted cheese is essential, but it is also something to watch when counting Points! If you decide to create your own variations, use a half-fat mozzarella cheese, finely grated, to help keep the Points low. Also, feel free to use as many different vegetables as you wish and use the Point-free Basic Tomato Sauce (page 6) – so much better than the ready-made pizza sauces in the supermarket which can be high in Points. Those of you who have time may want to prepare a batch of tomato sauce and then freeze it in useful quantities. Always cook pizzas on a heavy baking sheet in a preheated oven and serve them as soon as they come out of the oven.

Pasta is the other famous Italian contribution to the world's cuisine. Where would we be without it? It is quick and easy to make and can be prepared in so many different, delicious ways. Dried pasta is easy to store and cook but fresh pasta is a real treat and can be an even speedier option. The recipes here won't take up much of your time; all of them can be made in less than 30 minutes. There are so many pasta shapes and sizes available which means endless combinations and possibilities. Match up your favourites with the sauces in this book, which all have low Points and fresh, luscious flavours.

Basic Recipes

Here are four recipes to help you create quick, tasty pizzas and scrumptious bowls of pasta – all lower in Points and Calories than the average shop-bought or restaurant equivalents.

Basic Tomato Sauce

This sauce is suitable for both pizzas and pasta.

Preparation time: 5 minutes + 45 minutes cooking
Freezing: recommended
Points per serving: 0
Total Points per recipe: 0
Total Calories per recipe: 135

Ⓥ

2 × 400 g (14 oz) cans of chopped tomatoes
2 garlic cloves, crushed
3 artificial sweeteners
grated zest of ¹/₂ **lemon**
2 tablespoons chopped fresh parsley
salt and freshly ground black pepper

1 Place all the ingredients, except the parsley, in a saucepan.

2 Bring to the boil. Reduce the heat and simmer, uncovered, for 45 minutes, until the sauce is thick and pulpy. Add the parsley and leave to cool.

3 Purée in a blender or food processor for a smoother sauce or use as it is..

Chunky Tomato Sauce

Where would pasta be without tomato sauce? This one is extra good since it is full of chunks of vegetables.

Serves: 4
Preparation and cooking time: 35 minutes
Freezing: recommended
Points per serving: 0
Total Points per recipe: 0
Calories per serving: 55

Ⓥ

1 small onion, chopped finely
2 celery sticks, chopped finely (with leaves if
    possible)
1 carrot, chopped finely
3 tablespoons tomato purée
1 garlic clove, crushed
2 × 400 g (14 oz) cans of chopped tomatoes
125 ml (4 fl oz) tomato juice
150 ml (¹/₄ pint) vegetable stock
salt and freshly ground black pepper

❶ Put all the ingredients together in a large saucepan, bring to the boil and leave to simmer for 30 minutes, uncovered. Check the seasoning.

Basic Cheese Sauce

Cheese sauce is the delight of pasta lovers and this one has a hint of mustard for some extra flavour. Remember to add the Points for the pasta.

Serves: 4
Preparation and cooking time: 15 minutes
Freezing: recommended
Points per serving: 3
Total Points per recipe: 12
Calories per serving: 145

Ⓥ if using vegetarian cheese and margarine

1 tablespoon soft margarine
1 tablespoon plain flour
425 g (³/₄ pint) skimmed milk
100 g (3¹/₂ oz) half-fat Cheddar cheese, grated
¹/₂ teaspoon ready-made mustard
salt and freshly ground black pepper

❶ Melt the margarine in a large pan.
❷ Stir in the flour and cook for 2 minutes on a low heat, stirring all the time.
❸ Remove from the heat and gradually whisk in the milk.

❹ Return to the heat and bring to the boil, whisking constantly, until it thickens. Simmer for 3 minutes.
❺ Stir in the cheese, mustard and seasoning and stir until the cheese melts. Use as required.

Plain Scone Pizza Base

Use this as a base for any of the medium-size pizzas. Cook for the same length of time and at the same temperature as a pizza with a ready-made base. Use half the quantities to make a mini pizza.

Serves: 2

Preparation time: 15 minutes

Freezing: not recommended

Points per serving: with polyunsaturated
margarine 9; with hard margarine 10;
with butter 12

Total Points per recipe: with polyunsaturated
margarine 18; with hard margarine 20;
with butter 24

Calories per serving: 580

225 g (8 oz) white self-raising flour
50 g (1³/₄ oz) margarine or butter
150 ml (¹/₄ pint) skimmed milk
salt and freshly ground black pepper

ⓥ if using vegetarian margarine

❶ Sift the flour in a large bowl with the salt and pepper. Add the margarine or butter and rub in with your fingertips, until the mixture resembles fine breadcrumbs.

❷ Stir in the milk to form a soft dough. Turn out on to a lightly floured surface and knead gently.

❸ Roll out into a 20–25 cm (8–10 inch) round circle. Line a heavy baking sheet with baking parchment or greaseproof paper and transfer the pizza base to it.

Variation: stir 2 tablespoons of any chopped fresh herb or 1 tablespoon of any dried herb into the crumb mixture, before adding the milk.

Basic Cheese Sauce (page 7)
Chunky Tomato Sauce (page 7)
Plain Scone Pizza Base

Pizzas

I n this chapter you'll find pizzas to suit every taste.

   We start with the mini pizzas which are very quick to cook and great for just one person. You can use almost anything as a topping. As an alternative to shop-bought mini pizzas bases, use a mini pitta bread. (A mini pitta bread is 1 Point.)

   The medium-size thin and crispy pizzas serve two as a main course. Vegetarians and vegetable-lovers alike will enjoy the Vegetarian Pizza and the Margarita Pizza. The Four Seasons Pizza, the Tuna Pizza and the Asparagus and Ham Pizza are all wonderful blends of familiar and not-so-familiar flavours. Pizza Bianca is a tasty alternative to the usual garlic bread which can be served in slices with a salad or even with a pasta dish.

   Deep-pan pizzas are the all-time favourite with Americans, whereas the thin and crispy pizzas are more like the real thing in Italy. But thank goodness for deep-pan pizzas; they are thick, deeply satisfying and piled high with taste. The thicker base and sides of the deep-pan pizza form a shallow case which allows it to hold more topping. I have included some medium-size deep-pan pizzas, which serve two, and some large deep-pan pizzas which serve four.

Type of base	Serves	Points per serving	Total Points
Plain scone pizza base (page 8)	2	9–12	18–24
Mini pizza base*	1	$3^1/_2$	$3^1/_2$
Medium pizza base*	2	$3^1/_2$	7
Medium thin and crispy pizza base*	2	3	6
Medium deep-pan pizza base*	2	4	8
Large deep-pan pizza base*	4	$2^1/_2$	10

Use the Plain Scone Pizza Base recipe (page 8) if you want to make your own base for any of the pizzas, except the deep pan ones; otherwise, you can substitute any of the above which are available in the supermarket.

   Cook pizzas on a heavy baking sheet, lined with baking parchment or greaseproof paper, for a crisp base.

   *Points calculated for supermarket own-brand pizza bases.

Seasonings for Pizzas

For added flavour, as they come out of the oven, drizzle balsamic vinegar sparingly over any of the pizzas.

   Sprinkle any of the following seasonings over the cooked pizzas or add them instead of salt and freshly ground black pepper before cooking. None of these flavoured salts contain any Points.

   Chilli salt: grind one dried chilli with 3 tablespoons of coarse sea salt.

   Herb salt: grind one tablespoon of dried herb with 3 tablespoons of coarse sea salt. Choose from rosemary, thyme, basil, tarragon, mint or oregano.

Lemon or garlic salt: grind the finely grated zest of lemon with 2 tablespoons of coarse sea salt. Grind 3 garlic cloves with 3 tablespoons of coarse sea salt.

Hot peppers: grind one chopped dried chilli with 2 tablespoons of black peppercorns.

Light Garlic Bread

Nothing beats hot garlicky bread! This recipe lets you try it with a pizza base or pitta bread.

Serves: 1

Preparation time: 5 minutes + 10 minutes cooking

Freezing: recommended

Points per serving: 6 with pizza; 5 with pitta bread

Calories per serving: 300

Ⓥ

1 mini pizza base or medium-size pitta bread

1 tablespoon olive oil

1 garlic clove, crushed

❶ Preheat the oven to Gas Mark 5/190°C/375°F. Bake the pizza base for 10 minutes.

❷ Brush the olive oil on the base and top with the garlic. Serve warm.

Cook's note: brush the oil on to the cooked base with a pastry brush.

Variation: when using a pitta bread, just pop into the toaster and then add the oil and garlic when hot.

Italian Ham and Cheese Pizza

Figs and cottage cheese are refreshingly different toppings – pair this pizza with a tomato salad when you're in the mood for a change.

Serves: 1

Preparation time: 10 minutes + 10 minutes cooking

Freezing: not recommended

Points per serving: 5

Calories per serving: 310

1 mini pizza base
55 g (2 oz) diet plain cottage cheese, sieved
2 slices of wafer-thin ham
1 fresh fig, cut into wedges
6 watercress sprigs
salt and freshly ground black pepper

❶ Preheat the oven to Gas Mark 5/190°C/375°F.

❷ Spread the pizza base with cottage cheese.

❸ Top with the ham and fig wedges and bake for 10 minutes, until the crust is golden.

❹ Scatter over the watercress and seasoning to serve.

Variation: ripe pear can be used to replace the fig. Use ¹/₂ pear per pizza; remove the core and roughly chop the flesh.

Red Onion Pizza

Sweet red onions, garlic and basil topped with gooey mozzarella are a simple and tasty treat which you can enjoy either as a supper with a salad, or for lunch.

Serves: 1

Preparation time: 5 minutes + 20 minutes cooking

Freezing: recommended

Points per serving: 5¹/₂

Calories per serving: 285

¹/₂ large red onion, peeled and cut into wedges
1 garlic clove, chopped finely
1 tablespoon low-fat plain fromage frais
1 mini pizza base
3 fresh basil leaves or ¹/₂ teaspoon dried basil
15 g (¹/₂ oz) half-fat mozzarella cheese, grated
salt and freshly ground black pepper

❶ Preheat the oven to Gas Mark 5/190°C/375°F.

❷ Roast the onion wedges and garlic in a roasting tin for 10 minutes.

❸ Spread the fromage frais on the pizza base.

❹ Top with the roasted onion wedges and sprinkle on the basil and cheese.

❺ Bake for 10 minutes, until the cheese has melted and the crust is golden. Grind over the seasoning and serve at once.

Cook's note: to reheat a frozen pizza, thaw it first and then place it in an oven preheated to Gas Mark 5/190°C/375°F. Heat it for 5 minutes wrapped in foil and for 5 minutes without the foil.

Light Breakfast Pizza

Pizza for breakfast? Why not start the day with something to wake up your tastebuds – smoked salmon and fromage frais are a delicious alternative to toast and jam, and perfect for special occasions!

Serves: 1
Preparation time: 5 minutes + 10 minutes cooking
Freezing: not recommended
Points per serving: 6
Calories per serving: 300

1 mini pizza base
1 tablespoon chopped fresh coriander
2 tablespoons low-fat plain fromage frais
25 g (1 oz) smoked salmon, cut into strips
1 lemon wedge
freshly ground black pepper

1 Preheat the oven to Gas Mark 5/190°C/375°F.
2 Bake the pizza base for 10 minutes, until golden.
3 Mix together the coriander and fromage frais.

4 Top the warm base with the fromage frais and smoked salmon. Squeeze over the lemon juice and season with pepper.

Mini Tomato and Spinach Pizza

Pine kernels add a bit of flair to this delicious tomato and spinach topping.

Serves: 1
Preparation time: 5 minutes + 15 minutes cooking
Freezing: not recommended
Points per serving: 5
Calories per serving: 295

Ⓥ

1 mini pizza base
2 tablespoons Basic Tomato Sauce (page 6)
55 g (2 oz) spinach
55 g (2 oz) quark (low-fat soft cheese)
6 pine kernels
salt and freshly ground black pepper

1 Preheat the oven to Gas Mark 5/190°C/375°F.
2 Spread the pizza base with tomato sauce.
3 Wash the spinach and heat in a saucepan, until it wilts.

4 Top the tomato with the spinach, quark and pine kernels. Season well and bake for 15 minutes.

Margarita Pizza

The combination of tomato and basil is a favourite with Italians.

Serves: 2
Preparation time: 5 minutes + 15 minutes cooking
Freezing: not recommended
Points per serving: 5
Total Points per recipe: 10
Calories per serving: 205

1 medium-size thin and crispy pizza base
3 tablespoons Basic Tomato Sauce (page 6)
75 g (2³/₄ oz) ricotta cheese
1 tomato, sliced
1 tablespoon chopped fresh basil or 1 teaspoon
**   dried basil**

1 Preheat the oven to Gas Mark 7/220°C/425°F.

2 Spread the pizza base with tomato sauce. Sprinkle over the ricotta. Top with tomato slices and basil.

3 Bake for 15 minutes, until crisp.

Basil

Margarita Pizza
Asparagus and Ham Pizza (page 18)

Asparagus and Ham Pizza

A spring and summer delight when asparagus is in its prime. When you buy asparagus, make sure the buds are tight and the spears have an even colour and appear firm and unwrinkled.

Serves: 2
Preparation time: 5 minutes + 15 minutes cooking
Freezing: not recommended
Points per serving: 4$^1/_2$
Total Points per recipe: 9
Calories per serving: 220

4 fresh asparagus spears or 4 canned spears, each cut into 3 pieces
1 medium-size thin and crispy pizza base
2 tablespoons Basic Tomato Sauce (page 6)
1 tomato, sliced
50 g (1$^3/_4$ oz) half-fat mozzarella cheese, grated
$^1/_2$ teaspoon dried oregano
25 g (1 oz) wafer-thin slices of ham
salt and freshly ground black pepper

1 Preheat the oven to Gas Mark 7/220°C/425°F.

2 Boil the fresh asparagus for 3 minutes. Drain well and refresh under cold water. Drain again.

3 Spread the base with tomato sauce.

4 Top with the asparagus and tomato and then sprinkle over the cheese and oregano and top with ham.

5 Season well. Bake for 15 minutes, until crisp.

Vegetarian Pizza

This pizza is piled high with tasty vegetables but not with Calories: one of the great things about vegetables when you are trying to lose weight is that they are a no-Points food!

Serves: 2
Preparation time: 5 minutes + 25 minutes cooking
Freezing: not recommended
Points per serving: 7
Total Points per recipe: 14
Calories per serving: 310

Ⓥ

1 leek, sliced
1 courgette, sliced
1 onion, cut into thin wedges
1 tablespoon chopped fresh rosemary or
    1 teaspoon dried rosemary
3 tablespoons low-fat plain fromage frais
1 medium-size thin and crispy pizza base
    (suitable for vegetarians)
100 g (3¹/₂ oz) half-fat vegetarian mozzarella
    cheese, grated
salt and freshly ground black pepper

❶ Preheat the oven to Gas Mark 7/220°C/425°F.
❷ Mix the leek, courgette and onion in a shallow roasting tin. Roast for 15 minutes.
❸ Season well and stir in the rosemary.

❹ Spread fromage frais over the base. Top with the roasted vegetables and sprinkle with the cheese.
❺ Bake for 10 minutes, until crisp and golden. Season and serve as soon as possible.

Rosemary

Tuna Pizza

This is a nutritious and filling choice for a supper dish. Lots of texture and taste here.

Serves: 2
Preparation time: 5 minutes + 15 minutes cooking
Freezing: not recommended
Points per serving: 4½
Total Points per recipe: 9
Calories per serving: 270

1 medium-size thin and crispy pizza base
3 tablespoons Basic Tomato Sauce (page 6)
1 small onion, sliced
55 g (2 oz) mushrooms, sliced
100 g (3½ oz) can of tuna in water, drained and flaked
25 g (1 oz) sweetcorn kernels, or artichoke hearts, sliced (optional)
40 g (1½ oz) half-fat mozzarella cheese, grated
salt and freshly ground black pepper

1 Preheat the oven to Gas Mark 7/220°C/425°F.
2 Spread the pizza base with tomato sauce.
3 Top with the onion, mushrooms, tuna and sweetcorn or artichokes, if using. Sprinkle over the cheese and season.
4 Bake for 15 minutes, until crisp.

Neapolitan Pizza

This classic pizza from Naples has the rich and sensuous flavours of southern Italy.

Serves: 2
Preparation time: 10 minutes + 15 minutes cooking
Freezing: not recommended
Points per serving: 5½
Total Points per recipe: 11
Calories per serving: 275

½ × 55 g (2 oz) can of anchovies, drained
2 tablespoons milk
1 medium-size thin and crispy pizza base
3 tablespoons Basic Tomato Sauce (page 6)
½ teaspoon dried mixed Italian herbs
75 g (2¾ oz) half-fat mozzarella cheese, grated

1 Preheat the oven to Gas Mark 7/220°C/425°F.
2 Soak the anchovies in the milk for 10 minutes. Drain.
3 Spread the base with tomato sauce. Sprinkle over the herbs.
4 Sprinkle the cheese over the pizza base. Top with the anchovies and bake for 15 minutes.

Pizza Bianca

Here's something for garlic lovers. Simply scrumptious!

Serves: 2
Preparation time: 5 minutes + 10 minutes baking
Freezing: not recommended
Points per serving: 4¹/₂
Total Points per recipe: 9
Calories per serving: 185

Ⓥ

1 medium-size thin and crispy pizza base
1 tablespoon olive oil
3 garlic cloves, crushed

❶ Preheat the oven to Gas Mark 7/220°C/425°F.
❷ Brush ¹/₂ tablespoon of the oil over the base and bake for 10 minutes, or until crisp.
❸ Brush over the remaining oil and spread on the garlic.

Variation: add a teaspoon of one of the flavoured salts (pages 10–11).

Four Seasons Pizza

So many ingredients, so much flavour and such little effort!

Serves: 2
Preparation time: 5 minutes + 15 minutes cooking
Freezing: not recommended
Points per serving: 6¹/₂
Total Points per recipe: 13
Calories per serving: 295

1 medium-size thin and crispy pizza base
2 tablespoons Basic Tomato Sauce (page 6)
100 g (3¹/₂ oz) half-fat mozzarella cheese, grated
25 g (1 oz) mushrooms, sliced
1 tablespoon stoned black olives, sliced thinly
25 g (1 oz) spicy sausage, cut into matchsticks
¹/₂ teaspoon dried oregano
1 teaspoon capers
freshly ground black pepper

❶ Preheat the oven to Gas Mark 7/220°C/425°F.
❷ Spread the pizza base with tomato sauce.
❸ Sprinkle over the cheese. Top with mushrooms, olives, sausage, oregano and capers.

❹ Bake for 15 minutes. Season with pepper and serve hot.

Peperonata Pizza

When roasting these sweet peppers, don't worry about the charred skin – when it is peeled off, it leaves the pepper juicy with a heavenly, smoky flavour.

Serves: 3

Preparation time: 10 minutes + 25 minutes cooking

Freezing: recommended

Points per serving: 3½

Total Points per recipe: 10½

Calories per serving: 230

Ⓥ

1 red pepper, halved
1 yellow pepper, halved
1 small aubergine, sliced thinly
1 tablespoon chopped fresh thyme or 1 teaspoon dried thyme
1 medium-size deep-pan pizza base
6 tablespoons Basic Tomato Sauce (page 6)
75 g (2³/₄ oz) half-fat mozzarella cheese, grated

❶ Preheat the oven to Gas Mark 7/220°C/425°F.
❷ Place the peppers, cut-side down, on a heavy baking sheet, with the aubergine. Roast for 15 minutes.
❸ Rest the peppers by wrapping them in clingfilm or placing them in a polythene bag for 5 minutes.

Then remove the seeds and blackened skins. Cut the flesh into strips. Mix in the thyme.
❹ Spread the pizza base with tomato sauce. Top with aubergine slices and pepper strips. Sprinkle with cheese.
❺ Bake for 20 minutes until crisp.

Thyme

Peperonata Pizza

Spicy Prawn Pizza

Buy peeled and cooked prawns to save you time preparing this seafood delight with a bit of kick!

Serves: 3

Preparation time: 5 minutes + 18 minutes cooking

Freezing: not recommended

Points per serving: 4

Total Points per recipe: 12

Calories per serving: 225

1 medium-size deep-pan pizza base

6 tablespoons Basic Tomato Sauce (page 6)

100 g (3¹/₂ oz) peeled, cooked prawns

1 teaspoon Tabasco sauce or to taste

75 g (2³/₄ oz) half-fat mozzarella cheese, grated

¹/₂ teaspoon dried oregano

❶ Preheat the oven to Gas Mark 7/220°C/425°F.

❷ Spread the pizza base with tomato sauce.

❸ Mix together the prawns with Tabasco sauce to taste.

❹ Scatter the prawns over the base. Sprinkle over the mozzarella and oregano.

❺ Bake for 15–18 minutes, until crisp.

Oregano

Ham and Mushroom Pizza

Marinating the mushrooms in garlic and vinegar makes the great taste of ham and mushroom pizza even better.

Serves: 3

Preparation time: 5 minutes + 15 minutes
marinating + 18 minutes cooking

Freezing: not recommended

Points per serving: 3

Total Points per recipe: 9

Calories per serving: 155

100 g (3¹/₂ oz) field mushrooms, sliced
1 tablespoon red wine vinegar
1 garlic clove, crushed
1 medium-size deep-pan pizza base
3 tablespoons Basic Tomato Sauce (page 6)
25 g (1 oz) wafer-thin ham
25 g (1 oz) stoned black olives, sliced

❶ Preheat the oven to Gas Mark 7/220°C/425°F.

❷ Mix the mushrooms with the vinegar and garlic and marinate for 15 minutes.

❸ Spread the pizza base with tomato sauce. Drain the mushrooms and arrange them on top. Add the ham and olives and bake for 15–18 minutes, until crisp.

Hot and Spicy Pizza

Spice, spice and more spice in this pizza – definitely not for the fainthearted! If you're not keen on spicy food, reduce the quantity of chilli or leave it out altogether.

Serves: 4

Preparation time: 15 minutes + 25 minutes cooking

Freezing: not recommended

Points per serving: 5½

Total Points per recipe: 22

Calories per serving: 355

225 g (8 oz) extra-lean minced beef
2 tablespoons barbecue sauce
4 tablespoons tomato juice
6 tablespoons Basic Tomato Sauce (page 6)
1 large deep-pan pizza base
1 fresh red chilli, de-seeded and chopped finely
1 fresh green chilli, de-seeded and chopped finely
25 g (1 oz) spicy sausage, cut into matchsticks
75 g (2¾ oz) half-fat mozzarella cheese, grated

1 Preheat the oven to Gas Mark 7/220°C/425°F.

2 Heat a frying-pan and brown the mince for 2–3 minutes. Add the barbecue sauce and tomato juice and simmer for 10 minutes.

3 Spoon the tomato sauce on to the pizza base. Add the mince mixture.

4 Top with the chillies and spicy sausage and sprinkle over the cheese.

5 Bake for 20–25 minutes, until crisp. Serve immediately.

Chillies

Hot and Spicy Pizza

Marinara Pizza

The silvery anchovy has a deliciously strong and piquant flavour – here it is soaked in milk to remove some of the saltiness.

Serves: 4
Preparation time: 10 minutes + 25 minutes
  cooking
Freezing: not recommended
Points per serving: 3^1/$_2$
Total Points per recipe: 14
Calories per serving: 270

50 g (1³/₄ oz) can of anchovies, drained
2 tablespoons milk
1 large deep-pan pizza base
5 tablespoons Basic Tomato Sauce (page 6)
2 garlic cloves, crushed
100 g (3¹/₂ oz) can of tuna in brine, drained
    and flaked
2 tomatoes, sliced
1 teaspoon dried oregano
50 g (1³/₄ oz) stoned black olives, sliced

❶ Preheat the oven to Gas Mark 7/220°C/425°F.
❷ Soak the anchovies in the milk for 10 minutes.
❸ Meanwhile, spread the pizza base with tomato sauce. Scatter over the garlic and tuna. Top with

tomato slices, oregano and olives. Lastly, arrange the anchovies decoratively.
❹ Bake for 20–25 minutes, until crisp.

Mixed Vegetable Pizza

Eat healthily, and enjoy the textures and flavours of fresh vegetables along with sweetcorn which is high in carbohydrate and contains protein and vitamins A and C.

Serves: 4
Preparation time: 5 minutes + 20 minutes cooking
Freezing: not recommended
Points per serving: 3
Total Points per recipe: 12
Calories per serving: 245

Ⓥ if using vegetarian mozzarella

1 large deep-pan pizza base
6 tablespoons Basic Tomato Sauce (page 6)
2 garlic cloves, crushed
1 onion, sliced finely
50 g (1³/₄ oz) button mushrooms, sliced
1 small red pepper, de-seeded and sliced finely
1 small green pepper, de-seeded and sliced finely
1 tablespoon sweetcorn kernels
50 g (1¹/₂ oz) half-fat mozzarella cheese, grated

❶ Preheat the oven to Gas Mark 7/220°C/425°F.
❷ Spread the pizza base with tomato sauce.

❸ Top with garlic, onion, mushrooms, peppers and sweetcorn. Top with mozzarella and bake for 20 minutes, until crisp.

Pasta

Pasta has so much going for it. It is quick, easy to prepare and economical. It is also nourishing, easily digested, and releases energy over a long period of time. Best of all though, it has a low fat content, is very satisfying and tastes great.

When you are losing weight, watch the Points of the pasta sauce – it's the real culprit. With this in mind, I have created some tasty low-Point sauces for you to enjoy with any size or shape of pasta. I have included suggestions of pasta to accompany many of the sauces but please feel free to experiment and try your own variations and do remember to add the Points for the pasta in recipes which give Points for sauces only.

To make the pasta, allow 50 g (1³/₄ oz) of dried pasta per person and 75 g (2³/₄ oz) of fresh pasta per person. All packets of dried pasta carry clear cooking instructions but here are some standard instructions for your reference. Bring a large saucepan of water to a good rolling boil, add about 1 tablespoon of salt and toss in the pasta. (Pasta needs to be cooked in lots of boiling water so it can tumble freely and not stick together.) Bring the water and pasta back to the boil and cook for the recommended time. Drain immediately and tip straight back into the pan, so it is still slightly wet. Toss in the prepared sauce and mix well. Serve immediately.

Leek and Bacon Pasta Sauce

Leeks first appear in the autumn and early winter and are deservedly a much-loved vegetable. Their delicate flavour makes them the perfect accompaniment to savoury bacon in this pasta sauce. Serve with your favourite pasta shapes, remembering to add the Points.

Serves: 4
Preparation and cooking time: 25 minutes
Freezing: not recommended
Points per serving: 5¹/₂
Total Points per recipe: 22
Calories per serving: 200

1 quantity of Basic Cheese Sauce (page 7)
4 rashers of lean back bacon, cut into pieces
2 leeks, sliced
125 g (4 oz) broccoli, cut into small florets
salt and freshly ground black pepper

1 Make the cheese sauce.
2 Heat a large pan, add the bacon and leeks and fry for about 2 minutes.

3 Stir in the broccoli and cook for 2 minutes.
4 Add the cheese sauce, season to taste and gently simmer for 3 minutes.

Mushroom Pasta Sauce

This medley of mushrooms creates an intense savoury sauce. Mushrooms have a lot to offer; not only do they taste wonderful, they have low salt, no cholesterol and no fat! They also have lots of important vitamins and minerals. Serve with any pasta shape, remembering to add the Points.

Serves: 4

Preparation and cooking time: 25 minutes

Freezing: not recommended

Points per serving: 3

Total Points per recipe: 12

Calories per serving: 155

1 quantity of Basic Cheese Sauce (page 7)

50 g (1³/₄ oz) button mushrooms, chopped finely

75 g (2³/₄ oz) chestnut mushrooms, sliced or cut into wedges

100 g (3¹/₂ oz) field mushrooms, sliced

2 tablespoons chopped fresh parsley

ⓥ if using vegetarian Basic Cheese Sauce

❶ Make the cheese sauce, adding all the mushrooms to the melted margarine. Cook them for 2 minutes before adding the flour.

❷ Add the parsley and cheese.

Pasta Bows with Chicken and Sage Sauce

Sage flourishes in the Mediterranean where the heat of the sun concentrates its aromatic oils and makes it a lovely complement to other Mediterranean flavours. Here it is delicious with chicken and red wine.

Serves: 4
Preparation and cooking time: 20 minutes
Freezing: not recommended
Points per serving: 4¹/₂
Total Points per recipe: 18
Calories per serving: 310

225 g (8 oz) dried pasta bows
For the sauce:
2 medium-size boneless, skinless chicken
    breasts, cooked and cut into bite-size pieces
1 small onion, chopped finely
1 tablespoon chopped fresh sage
125 ml (4 fl oz) red wine
3 tablespoons low-fat plain fromage frais
salt and freshly ground black pepper

❶ Place the chicken, onion and sage in a frying-pan, with the red wine. Simmer, uncovered, for 10 minutes.

❷ Meanwhile, cook the pasta according to the packet instructions. Drain.

❸ Mix the chicken mixture, pasta and fromage frais together. Season and serve immediately.

Farfalle

Red Pepper Pesto and Cannelloni

Cannelloni is Italian comfort food – it can be stuffed with such tasty and filling ingredients.
In this recipe it oozes with cheese, red peppers and aubergines.

Serves: 4

Preparation time: 25 minutes + 20 minutes baking

Freezing: not recommended

Points per serving: 2

Total Points per recipe: 8

Calories per serving: 345

V if using vegetarian ricotta

2 red peppers, halved

1 aubergine, chopped roughly

2 unpeeled garlic cloves

**2 tablespoons chopped fresh basil or 2 teaspoons
    dried basil**

50 g (1³/₄ oz) fresh white breadcrumbs

75 g (2³/₄ oz) ricotta cheese, crumbled

freshly grated nutmeg

For the cannelloni:

12 cannelloni tubes

1 quantity of Chunky Tomato Sauce (page 7)

1 Preheat the oven to Gas Mark 7/220°C/425°F.

2 Place the peppers, cut-side down, with the aubergine and garlic on a heavy baking tray and roast in the oven for 10 minutes, until the pepper skins are well blackened.

3 Cover the peppers and garlic with clingfilm or put in a polythene bag and leave to cool. Peel the peppers and remove the seeds. Peel the roasted garlic.

4 Place the pepper flesh, garlic and basil in a food processor and blend until smooth. Stir in the breadcrumbs, aubergine and ricotta and season with nutmeg.

5 Stuff this mixture into cannelloni tubes, place in a baking dish and top with tomato sauce. Bake for 20 minutes, until the pasta is soft.

Variation: cook 225 g (8 oz) dried pasta shapes, according to the packet instructions. Add to the aubergine mixture and tomato sauce in a large saucepan and heat through. Points will be 3¹/₂ per serving.

Red Pepper Pesto and Cannelloni
Pasta Bows with Chicken and Sage Sauce (page 35)

Chinese Pasta with Cucumber Relish

Some say it wasn't the Italians who invented pasta, but the Chinese. Capelli is fine, long spaghetti which is probably not unlike the original Chinese pasta which evolved into the well-known noodle. Capelli is often sold in small, nest-like bunches and is mouth-watering with these oriental flavours.

Serves: 4
Preparation and cooking time: 25 minutes
Freezing: not recommended
Points per serving: 3
Total Points per recipe: 12
Calories per serving: 275

225 g (8 oz) capelletti pasta
3 spring onions, chopped finely
2.5 cm (1-inch) piece of fresh root ginger, peeled and grated
1 garlic clove, crushed
2 tablespoons light soy sauce
2 tablespoons dry sherry
175 g (6 oz) peeled, cooked prawns
For the relish:
1/2 cucumber, cut into small cubes
1 red pepper, de-seeded and chopped finely
finely grated zest and juice of 1 lime
salt and freshly ground black pepper

❶ Cook the pasta in a large pan of salted, boiling water.
❷ Place the onions, ginger, garlic, soy sauce and sherry in a wok or large frying-pan and simmer for 3 minutes.
❸ Meanwhile, make the relish and mix the cucumber, pepper, lime zest and juice together and season well.

❹ Add the prawns to the onion mixture and heat for 2 minutes.
❺ Drain the pasta and mix with the prawn mixture.
❻ Serve the pasta in bowls, with a tablespoon of cucumber relish on top.

Variation: add a fresh red chilli, de-seeded and finely chopped, instead of the pepper, for a hotter relish.

Pasta Shells with Salmon and Salsa

Intensely aromatic peppercorns, salmon steak and coriander fill these pasta shells with loads of flavour.

Serves: 4
Preparation and cooking time: 20 minutes
Freezing: not recommended
Points per serving: 3¹/₂
Total Points per recipe: 14
Calories per serving: 310

225 g (8 oz) dried pasta shells
For the sauce:
225 g (8 oz) salmon steak
1 lemon
1 bay leaf
3 peppercorns
4 tomatoes, chopped roughly
¹/₂ red onion, chopped finely
finely grated zest and juice of 1 lime
2 tablespoons chopped fresh coriander
salt and freshly ground black pepper

❶ Place the salmon steak in a small pan with the juice of the lemon. Add the bay leaf, peppercorns and 3 tablespoons of water. Cook, covered, for 10 minutes. Leave in the hot water once cooked.

❷ Meanwhile, cook the pasta shells in salted boiling water, according to the packet instructions.

❸ Drain the salmon, remove the bones and skin and break up the flesh into large flakes.

❹ Heat the salmon flakes, tomatoes, red onion, lime zest and juice together for 5 minutes. Stir in the coriander and season well.

❺ Drain the pasta, mix it with the sauce and serve.

Conchiglie

Pasta Shells with Salmon and Salsa
Crab and Vegetable Pasta (page 42)

Crab and Vegetable Pasta

Very similar to fettuccine, tagliatelle are flat, ribbon noodles with a lovely thickness. If you want to spice up the mild flavour of crabmeat, try the sauce variation below.

Serves: 4
Preparation and cooking time: 20 minutes
Freezing: not recommended
Points per serving: 3½
Total Points per recipe: 14
Calories per serving: 265

225 g (8 oz) tagliatelle
2 courgettes, cut into thin ribbons
2 carrots, peeled and cut into thin ribbons
100 g (3½ oz) can of crabmeat, drained and flaked
4 tablespoons low-fat plain fromage frais
2 tablespoons tomato ketchup
salt and freshly ground black pepper

❶ Cook the tagliatelle for 12 minutes in salted, boiling water. Drain.

❷ Meanwhile, blanch the vegetables for 2 minutes in salted, boiling water; drain well. Mix with the crabmeat, fromage frais and tomato ketchup, season well and gently heat for 3 minutes.

❸ Mix with the pasta and serve.

Variation: add 1 extra tablespoon of fromage frais and a fresh red chilli, de-seeded, instead of the tomato ketchup, for a hotter sauce. Points will remain the same.

Pasta Quills with Tuna and Tomato Sauce

Always have some canned tuna on hand – it's so versatile and inexpensive. Tuna belongs to the same fish family as mackerel and is full of goodness. And pasta loves it, hot or cold.

Serves: 4
Preparation and cooking time: 20 minutes
Freezing: not recommended
Points per serving: 2¹/₂
Total Points per recipe: 10
Calories per serving: 255

225 g (8 oz) dried pasta quills
For the sauce:
1 small onion, chopped roughly
4 fresh tomatoes, chopped roughly
150 ml (¹/₄ pint) tomato juice
**175 g (6 oz) fresh spinach, washed, or frozen
   spinach, thawed**
100 g (3¹/₂ oz) can of tuna in brine, drained
salt and freshly ground black pepper

❶ Place the onion, tomatoes and tomato juice in a saucepan and simmer, uncovered, for 10 minutes, stirring from time to time.
❷ Add the spinach and tuna and cook for a further 5 minutes. Season well.

❸ Meanwhile, cook the pasta in salted, boiling water, according to the packet instructions.
❹ Drain the pasta, mix with the tuna sauce and serve.

Penne

43

Tagliatelle with Garlic and Mushroom Sauce

Deliciously creamy and low in Points!

Serves: 4
Preparation and cooking time: 20 minutes
Freezing: not recommended
Points per serving: 2¹/₂
Total Points per recipe: 10
Calories per serving: 225

225 g (8 oz) green tagliatelle
75 g (2³/₄ oz) open-cup mushrooms, sliced
100 ml (3¹/₂ fl oz) vegetable stock
75 g (2³/₄ oz) low-fat garlic soft cheese
2 tablespoons chopped fresh parsley
salt and freshly ground black pepper

V if using vegetarian cream cheese

1 Cook the pasta in salted, boiling water for 2 minutes. Drain well.
2 Cook the mushrooms in the stock for 3 minutes.

3 Stir in the garlic cheese and parsley. Add the pasta and heat gently for 2 minutes. Season and serve.

Pasta Twists with Light Pesto Sauce

In Italy pesto is known as 'food for the Gods'.

Serves: 4
Preparation and cooking time: 20 minutes
Freezing: not recommended
Points per serving: 3¹/₂
Total Points per recipe: 14
Calories per serving: 255

225 g (8 oz) dried pasta twists
For the sauce:
20 fresh basil leaves or 1 teaspoon dried basil
1 red onion, peeled and chopped roughly
2 tablespoons balsamic vinegar
150 ml (¹/₄ pint) half cream
salt and freshly ground black pepper

V

1 Cook the pasta in salted, boiling water for 12 minutes. Drain.
2 In a food processor, process the basil, onion and vinegar together until smooth.

3 Mix the pesto, pasta and cream together and heat gently for 3 minutes. Season and serve.

Tagliatelle with Garlic and Mushroom Sauce

Pasta Bows with Mustardy Chicken Sauce

Nothing beats a tasty cream sauce with pasta, and mustard and chicken, together with the luxuriously soft texture of leeks, make this dish very moreish indeed!

Serves: 4
Preparation and cooking time: 20 minutes
Freezing: not recommended
Points per serving: 4
Total Points per recipe: 16
Calories per serving: 285

225 g (8 oz) dried pasta bows
750 ml (1½ pints) chicken stock
2 medium-size, skinless, boneless chicken breasts, cooked and cut into bite-size pieces
1 garlic clove, crushed
2 leeks, chopped finely
2 teaspoons whole-grain mustard
2 tablespoons half cream
freshly ground black pepper

1 Cook the pasta in the chicken stock. Drain, reserving the stock.

2 Meanwhile, place the chicken, garlic, leeks and mustard in a saucepan, add 200 ml (7 fl oz) of chicken stock from the cooking of the pasta and gently simmer for 5 minutes, uncovered.

3 Stir the cream into the sauce and heat for 2 minutes, uncovered. Season with black pepper and serve with the pasta.

Rotini

Pasta Bows with Mustardy Chicken Sauce

Index